A Skeptic's outlook on Bitcoin

Brief words on the early indications of a calamity

By

Valentin Kugler

Introduction

Virtual currencies are digital substitutes to what most are familiar with as the monetary system, such instruments are useful, sound tools to be used in everyday transactions if applied in small groups, limited to an insignificant portion of the global population, however over the past few years some have reached a state where their name rings a bell in people's ear all around the globe. They are used to conduct nameless transactions, similar to real money, except majority of the exchanges are either strictly digital, or of questionable intent, and the ones that aren't, still depend on the vendor providing the goods or services. This being said, the businessman generally doesn't have a reason to use cryptic currencies instead of Benjamins, making the sole benefits of doing so any of three things, increasing the size of one's consumer base, satisfying the need to run with the herd, or to evade the long arm of the law. The past performance of cryptocurrencies has been outstanding, seamless, in less than half a decade they went from not being heard of at all, to having an aggregated monetary value of over $124 Billion (To emphasize the magnificence of this, in the past year S&P 500's price increased by 16%, DJIA's by 22%, the most popular coin's by 628%). Why and how does something accomplish such great performance, and where does the capital that funds these machines come from? Questions similar to this are the reason this piece of literature exists.

It is already obvious that something isn't quite right here, this is what is usually referred to as a "speculative bubble", and we have all heard about them at least once beforehand. Every time a bubble collapses, we assume that the next one will be prevented by the all-seeing & all-knowing finance people we know so well, up until it actually happens again – of course. Why aren't they prevented? The answer to that question is greed, and choosing to turn a blind eye to the problem instead of solving it. In most ordinary cases this is the answer, but with Bitcoin there is another factor to it, that it is not a stock market bubble, and has been one of very few non-stock market ones in the past few centuries. There have been many lessons learnt by people and institutions who lost money on speculative securities, and have decided

Introduction

to take a more conservative route ever since, but cryptic currencies are something not many people understand, and forget to apply the same principles and precautions to them as they would with companies.

There are many small pieces that help us understand the workings of cryptocurrencies, turning it from just a string of numbers, to something that is appealing to many, and appalling to few all around the world, it is quite difficult to put it into words without being either incoherent, or overly brief, however I will attempt to do so in a manner that is understandable by people who are not particularly familiar with the usage of financial terms. All my life I have been fascinated with emerging markets, from a young age I practically made it my goal to see every craze from the perspective of the people responsible for such acts, this lead me to study different market behaviors whenever I could, if possible I would do it by myself, but oftentimes I turned to books written by great economists and investors who have had much more experience than me, with this stated, it will be apparent to the reader that I am not trying to downplay the infrastructure or complexity of such systems, even I recognize the impressiveness of it, what I am attempting to accomplish is to shed light on the potential misuse, abuse, weaknesses of such works. Whenever the word ''cryptocurrency'' is said in this book, it will most likely be in reference to ''Bitcoin'', one of the oldest, and currently biggest form of cryptic currencies, making the culprit the greatest example to use thorough, but even though they may be interchangeable in most cases, when cryptocurrencies are mentioned it is not strictly about Bitcoin (even if Bitcoin is mentioned, it is still not strictly about Bitcoin), and is mostly used as an umbrella, or a beautiful blanket term to describe several others.

Analysis

In order to capture the inner balance of Bitcoin, I will sort its qualities into certain categories, compare it to other forms of securities (Companies, Bonds, Commodities, Real Estate, etc.), and eventually propose certain procedures which could let us improve the behavior of such instruments. Most cryptocurrencies are bought for their purchasing power, which is rather unique and unfamiliar to the financial world, that purchasing power greatly relies on governments not interfering with it in any form, but if things wouldn't go as planned, we would most likely see replacements for it appear, since when something gets abolished, and people want it enough, someone, somewhere will still find a way to fulfill those needs in some manner, which in this case would be replicating Bitcoin, giving it the same purpose, and expecting similar results from it.

Backing

Ordinary securities derive their value from an underlying asset that they represent, making them relatively easy to view from a factual perspective to analyze them, unlike cryptocurrencies. Stocks' price corresponds to the value of the company they represent, futures claim their value through commodities, the dollar bill got it from gold up until 1971, ever since then it was backed by the full faith and credit of the U.S. government, however Bitcoin receives it from the faith of its consumer base, and less known, but more importantly; its purchasing power. The problem with it relying on faith is similar to standing in a circle, holding hands and committing to a "leap o' faith" collectively... if one person doesn't fully commit, or missteps, the strength of it will be decreased drastically. One might say that even with other forms of securities, the value is just what we give to it, and that is true to a certain extent, but many valuable commodities have real life uses, for example wheat is used to make food, giving it more inherent value than say stones or metals, however as more human needs become satisfied, the more prominent the need for bricks and gold becomes, technically putting pleasure at the top, some of which can only be fulfilled through

Analysis

questionable ways.

Profitability and Growth

The most accessible way to tell how a company is doing is to look at their past performance, with Bitcoin and most other well-known cryptocurrencies, prior growth has been something one couldn't have even dreamt of, outperforming almost every other option one could have chosen, to visualize the magnificence of it, in the past year S&P 500's price increased by 16%, DJIA's by 22%, Bitcoin's by 628%. Some of the less experienced people may think that such trend cannot be stopped, but as the old saying goes; our hindsight is 20/20, but our foresight is legally blind, unfortunately this also applies to cryptocurrencies. The only redeeming analytical quality of Bitcoin is its previous growth (though to contrarian investors it may make it seem less desirable because of its price), while with general securities, people that devoted their college years to developing a clear understanding of variety of data, make sure that they are worthwhile investments, causing them to be strictly scrutinized, but the opposite is true for cryptic currencies, knowing their intrinsic value has been proved to be extremely difficult, impossible. See, others offer features such as dividends, voting rights, a strong fundamental background, or the security to sell a contract at a its price, and go on to buy the commodity it represents without worrying about extreme differences that may appear in prices, making you practically able to have a barrel of crude oil delivered to your doorstep, in exchange for your contract. Investing in virtual currencies could be likened to doing so with real-life ones, especially emerging ones, viewing it in that way would require us to look at growth in the past decades with adequate supplementary documentation, however there is not only insufficient data, the rollercoaster of Bitcoin has taken several trips down south for little to no reason.

Stability and Volatility

If there is something Bitcoin is notorious for, it is its volatility, since there is no fundamental baseline that would encourage people to purchase if the

Analysis

price went below such guideline, and sell if it went above. Cryptocurrencies are a rather newfound way of spending your money, it is still quite unclear for even the brightest minds to estimate one's value. There have been several foolish attempts at guesstimating the future value of Bitcoin, outrageous numbers such as $5 Trillion for market capitalization (For reference the aggregate of all coins and paper bills is $5T aswell), and on the other side of the spectrum, predictions of it never being used again, which is also very unlikely since it holds the power to purchase things outside the reach of the government (Which will be spoken about in greater detail later on). There are some ways with which we could mitigate such issues, but none of them are pretty... one being establishing an internal body to continuously exchange coins for real valuables, such as gold, minerals or arctic icebergs, whichever you choose, as long as it is a security or resource which possesses a relatively stable price, you establish backing with, however having a governing body could cripple the inherent motive behind cryptocurrencies.

Inherent Nature

This segment will be less on rock solid analytic and facts, and more on sociology and rough assumptions supplied by a line of reasoning, for example there being an abundance of speculators involved in the trading of crypto, since Bitcoin for example doesn't give us a way to fundamentally analyze it, leaving us only two options technical and event-based trading, and the former option heavily relies on speculation. I am also going to assume that the Crypto-heavyweight spends quite a bit of time in front of a computer, since the currency is more accepted in tech-y circles, and the chance of being exposed to such thing increases linearly with time being spent on the web. With the first fact I am going to turn back the topic of volatility, the people who rely on technical analysis more than fundamental, generally tend to overtrade, be more impatient, and while this phenomenon also exists in other markets, they give us other options to turn profits, rather than just crude guessing. On the latter fact, I wanted to make the point that such people start experiencing the mere-exposure effect that advertisements tend to put on you, making you more likely to be convinced that such thing

Analysis

is a viable instrument for you to put your money into, unfortunately this also gives people who want to do wrong the power to influence you.

Low volume

Cryptocurrencies often experience a state in which they trade in extremely low volumes (~0.1% of MKT Cap a day), from which we can come to the conclusion that a significant portion of users don't utilize their ability to purchase things, only sitting on it to use as an "investment". Volume is essentially the lube that keeps the machine of trading operating smoothly, following the rules of Supply and Demand, however with there being few entities which are being exchanged, causes prices to follow abnormal behavior. This statement may seem to weaken the point I made in the previous paragraph, but I would consider the portion that is being traded for no good reason to be unnecessary, while it does increase the turnover on paper, it doesn't motivate the others to trade theirs for services, and neither does it attempt to achieve the equilibrium price, therefore we should always be working to eliminate such phenomenon. This may become more prominent later on, as coins have a way of getting left behind, similar to pennies in real life. While it certainly is not a good idea to forget about them intentionally, there are many ways this can be caused, if a person who has accumulated great amounts of Bitcoin passes away, had they not left their sensitive information in their will, those keys will be stuck in the void forever, another possibility of this happening is as companies start circulating more cryptic currencies, and they are not careful enough with their handling, coins may be left in the wallets of employees who do not particularly celebrate the usage of such systems.

Miscellaneous Weaknesses / Risks

There are some hypothetical scenarios which could cause the value of coins to be diminished, and if such were to happen, it could diminish coins' value severely, and could function as a crash before the one where people come to a collective conclusion that such investments may not have been the greatest of ideas, after all.

Analysis

One of such scenarios would be a coin holding site starting to unknowingly function as a fractional reserve system, lending out more coins than it actually owns, all it would take is a savvy programmer who desires to make a dime. Previously the abolishment of such systems has been considered with real-life banks, especially after the great depression and after recent recession experienced after the Real Estate shenanigan. Historically, conservative ways of handling money become the general practice after market crashes and capitalism outworking itself, and when the economy is working at full force, more liberal methods are employed (such as fractional reserve banking) to cause slight inflation all the while having more money in circulation, the current state of coin trading seems to be extremely healthy from an economical perspective, practically firing on all 8 cylinders, so if one was to employ such methods covertly, they could cause great damage if it goes unnoticed for a great lengths of time.

The second possible case would be if "Satoshi", the alleged creator, and first user of Bitcoin would decide to let go of the coins in his wallet. This wouldn't inherently affect the value of the currency, however with everyone seeing others' transactions (Thanks to the public ledger), he wouldn't be able to offload them in secrecy, similar to employees of publicly-traded companies, along with major stake holders. Most "insiders" have to file a notice a certain amount of time before they can complete the transaction, immobilizing them from selling their shares at the ring o' bad news, or buying every for sale share in the public's hand in case they win a big government contract, alternatively, if find a crashed UFO in one of the factories. To forge it all into words, imagine if Warren Buffet, or JP Morgan decided to start buying large quantities of AAPL, of course the price would soar and everyone would want to follow the trend generated by two trustworthy names. Now in reverse, those guys start selling AAPL's stock, the same thing would happen with the opposite effect… this is what would happen if the first user would sell even a fraction of a coin, since such behavior is unexpected, and unfamiliar to everyone in the user base.

Analysis

Comparison to further securities

Bonds

A high yield corporate bond has the ability to yield 7-8% in 12 months to its owner, and while that may sound good to some, it is practically nothing compared to the performance of leading cryptos, as mentioned before, Bitcoin grew 628% comparative to last year, and several newfound ones went from a few cents to a couple of dollars in the matter of months. Another redeeming advantage that Cryptocurrencies have is that they are untaxed (if you want), similar to US Treasury bonds, in very different manners, which yield only 5% annually. You may be wondering as to why anyone in their right minds would choose to purchase bonds instead of something that grew hundred times its own size, in less than a year, something you have just discovered thanks to the internet. The reason for doing so could be explained in one word: safety. Bonds are backed by the company or the country, and if something bad happened, for example they don't pay out, you can practically in a twisted manner walk into their office and take (almost) anything your eyes desire, all the while cryptocurrencies are unpredictable, volatile, and wild.

Stocks

In the past year, S&P (16.45%), NASDAQ (21.56%), and DJIA (23.29%) grew 20.43% on average, which is starting to look closer to the desired figure of 628%. While indexes are still extremely good investment decisions, they are merely backed by the companies behind them, and your ability to choose the right ones. Common stocks are one of the greatest comparable securities to what we are witnessing at this very moment, there were always segments getting overpriced in the market, but stocks have achieved the greatest amounts of such happenings. We have over a dozen speculative bubbles under our belt, which affected thousands of companies, and several millions of persons each, they have had books written about them, describing in great detail how and what caused them, the ways we

Analysis

could prevent it from happening ever again, unfortunately people always seem to forget the teachings of others when it goes against their current motives.

Real life currencies

At first I was going to compare one of the most stable currencies (Swiss Francs - CHF) to the currencies used by leading nations (USD – EUR – JPY), but as one could have guessed from previous statements of mine, currencies don't behave in the same manner as other securities, they are relative to each other in a greater sense. It also has to be noted that some currencies are still backed by a good, making them essentially worth as much as their representative commodity.

Surprisingly, similar to cryptic currencies, even the most well-known currencies have struggled quite a bit to achieve an inner balance amongst themselves, the American government fought tooth-and-nail to make paper money be accepted by merchants, transitioning from silver & golden coins, and even those beautiful coins had their very own problems, when they were first being minted, sailors more often than not took a batch of silver dollars with themselves to foreign nations, and as natives took notice of the new shiny freedom coins, they wanted to exchange the heavier silver coin found around those areas, in exchange for the U.S. dollar coin. After all, the coins got lost in the crowd overseas, and newly landed coins were to be defaced and taken to the U.S. mint to be melted; turning foreign coins into American ones. Not to mention that often there were fluctuations in the price, thanks to new locations being found in which silver is abundantly present, along with the extremely high demand the U.S. government created for precious metals, so the state found it difficult to achieve equilibrium, the right amount of metal to use for the coins, and overall to not end up losing money on forging coinage.

Analysis

Commodities

Commodities and cryptocurrencies follow the same principles when it comes to handling them, but they also differ greatly in other areas. The first of the likesomeness arises from the fact that when you buy a Bitcoin or a bar of gold, you are actually buying it, and can probably expect it to stay where you left it, unlike shares of a company which can get split or spoiled by the way how that company handles business. Second being is that they are purchased in greater volumes when prices are expected to rise, this can also be assumed for cryptocurrencies even though they have a very short track record for us to study, however based on other resemblances we can only assume it to be this way, for example precious metals are more likely to be bought when people are expecting economic downturns in their country, or if a huge gold deposit was found, increasing the supply so greatly that prices would inflate severely, and with bitcoin; prices decrease if the chance of it being made illegal becomes more prominent, or the prices soar if the demand for certain hard-to-get products turns plentiful.

Conclusion

Cryptocurrencies are time bombs if not treated with proper care and scrutiny, bubbles comparable to the tulip craze of the 17th century, in which affluent merchants bought tulips (and mutations of certain) to flaunt their wealth, and in the same manner, cryptocurrencies are often bought to fit in with a certain group, such actions can be malevolent, if it's not purchased for its utility. A crisis to liken it to would be the dotcom boom, since both of them share similar qualities, they were still fairly new, and no one had a clear idea as to how to analyze them (A technological company's SEC filings will look completely different from a firm that operates in a different industry), and that they both turned out to be overvalued later on. The only person that can prevent bubbles is you, if you follow data instead of the words of charlatans, and others do aswell, you can save yourself from the heartache and financial loss that accompanies a crash, one must learn from historical events, and strive to not repeat them. As with all speculative disasters, greed is the main mover of cryptic currencies, nobody wants to

Analysis

miss out on the newest way to get rich, one would assume that with all the crisis we have experienced in the past few decades we would collectively be able to prevent them from ever happening again, however contrary to popular belief it is not the all-seeing institutions that are the biggest movers of the market, and even if they are, they are not any more cautious than your average person, they often have gains to make to keep their appearances up just like you, feeble-minded human, who feels like whose friends would bully if you didn't cash out with the newest opportunity right in front of your beautiful eyes.

While from an analytical standpoint it seems undesirable, from an investor's eye, owning them in moderate amounts (less than 1% of complete portfolio) could benefit the holder in case prices keep on ascending, and not cause much headache if it packed its bags and left for Mexico the next day. An overlooked aspect of investing, and in this case, cryptocurrency, is that we as humans care a lot about what our money is doing, so if one was to place their money in it, they may spend so much time looking at it, that they could have doubled their investment just by doing work instead, or improving themselves in a way or another, being free of the gruesome worry is often worth the extra precautions. While being overly careful may result in you seeing a security's price go up so much that you regret not buying it, or selling before it hit its highest point, but it is better to leave the table with a single chip, compared to none at all. As enough time passes, almost all currently known companies will go out of business, and get replaced, rendering their representative derivative worthless, but this should not cause you to be indecisive, since with enough learning, you can gain the ability to weed the bad ones out, and remember the meaning of the old saying, that the weakness doesn't exist in the securities, but in ourselves.

Socioeconomic – Political Effects

Caused by the narrow variety of options one has when attempting to exchange their newly acquired Bitcoins for something else, they often have to turn to illegal goods and services, potentially increasing the amount of drug users, thereby non-violent crimes, if they do not liquidate it for real money instead. Such obstacles draw bad attention to cryptic currencies from leaderships, some may even prohibit the use of cryptic currencies in an attempt to hinder the number of illegal transactions being conducted, increasing the amount of taxable trade, or theoretically, to gain some form of political advantage in one way or another, such measures incrementally minimize ways for criminals to carry out business, making them less motivated to go on with each currency's power being diminished, but doing so re-employs the low-level drug dealers once again, motivating the producers of drugs in one's own country, since the competition from outside entities is decreased tremendously. At the time of writing, four countries have regulated the use of cryptic currencies, one for political & authorian reasons, to not let such currencies draw away from the strength of the country's currency, Bangladesh has taken notice of its ability to launder money and has gone forward to take the matter into its own hands, while the other two banned it for being an unstable investment, which is potentially detrimental to the people in those countries, several headlines of articles about this piece of legislature explicitly stated that the governing bodies of Kyrgyzstan & Bolivia labeled Bitcoin an "unstable investment" & "Pyramid scheme", both of which we have to agree with at this point and time, the very basis of it operates as a Ponzi scheme, where people get return on their investments up until the point where it is no longer sustainable. Another great perspective on the mindset of cryptocurrency consumers could be attributed to the "castle-in-the-air" theory coined by John Maynes Keynes, the idea of it is that anything is a great investment as long as someone else is willing to pay more for it, while extremely effective if used by the right hands, I would deem such methods of creating wealth unethical to a certain degree, and not something a run-of-the-mill financial analyst should use. The few scenarios where such "psychological warfare" may be useful is if someone finds an already undervalued section in the market, and realizes that sometime in the future there will be changes made to another industry which will require high demand from the initial section we have mentioned, thinking in a similar manner may cause one to get better results since he or she has a wider and more detailed view of the possible investment they might make, making them more prone to finding great opportunities.

Government Relations

The greatest threat to the perceived value of cryptic currencies is the possibility that legislature may be passed against them, which could cause their usage to be severely restricted, or perhaps completely ceased. As mentioned previously, governing bodies have several reasons to scrutinize, examine the behavior of cryptocurrenices, and its users. The amount of taxes evaded by sneaky persons is enough to build a great school, or a monument that could enrichen a city even, and while the income gained by selling illicit goods would most likely go untaxed anyway, it would still be kept in circulation, spent on goods of non-criminal use, benefitting the economy to a considerable degree. One of the most common moral uses of cryptic currencies is employing it to avoid unnecessary government intervention, confiscation of property, when using services, and committing acts that are already heavily scrutinized by the law, such as VPNs (which enable you to protect your anonymity to a great degree), tipping journalists that highlight discuss risky topics, and transporting money to far-away countries. I am glad that we are able to do such things, being able to avoid tyranny, and an overly authorian state. If the people couldn't keep the state in check – by turning to such methods – it would be the sign of something really bad going on, however doing it without a great reason can cause the bond between the country and its citizens to deteriorate.

Cryptocurrencies ease the difficulty of conducting risky transactions, making it assist crime, drug usage, weapon trafficking and the spreading sensitive adult materials, by cutting out the middleman, the people in need of illegal goods can go right to the supplier. If the widespread usage of cryptic currencies becomes the norm, we all would be accessories to crime, and its detrimental social effects. There are many people who wouldn't otherwise touch drugs, but are either pressured by a group to try them, or are not mentally strong enough to keep themselves from it, with Bitcoin being widespread, otherwise reputable, successful people may fall to the call of narcotics, causing demise in their lives & society. All along with enterprising criminals getting connected to the network, being able to access weaponry, with which they could commit heinous crimes, create conflict, and cause law-abiding people to feel threatened in a by-law gun free / heavily regulated society.

Potential Government Involvement

In case the government doesn't want to completely cease the usage of cryptocurrencies, they may try to tame the beast themselves, by supervising the usage of it. While seemingly unlikely, there are many eastern countries using Bitcoins in some way, similar to how they secretly spy on people, it may not be honorable, but being able to wire money namelessly has great advantages to people in the position of power aswell. The destiny of cryptocurrencies would be similar to what we see as normal money today, if it was to go on similar to this scenario, it would be heavily regulated in use, including the marketplaces where it is allowed to be used, and if such was to happen, the leaderships could not only take the ability to buy questionable things online, but our data and information would most likely be threatened as well. If the knowledge we have is stripped of us, we are powerless once again, since our minds are one of the very few things that we cannot be taken of us, however if we cannot learn from other people, we can't accumulate great knowledge either. Leading away, it becomes obvious that if any of this was ever to happen, not only would it be opposed to the inherent motive, spirit behind cryptocurrencies, it could cause change in an undesirable direction.

Increased "quiet" crime

With the middlemen and other low-ranking members of criminal organization becoming not necessary to sell drugs anymore, the rate of violent crimes relating to drug trade and other miscellaneous illegal activities could drop significantly, while the volume of illicit goods being moved around increases, with less attention from authorities, even the more prominent criminals could stay outside the perspective of the law. Previously if one wanted to acquire forged documents, or disappear in a way or another, they had to do it themselves using crude methods, trying their luck doing it at home, or visiting someone who may know someone proficient at doing it, passing the information up to the person who is familiar with such practices, and working the transaction out with them using the middle man. Now the preferred practice is sending a specified amount of Bitcoin to an address, along with a photo, some supplementary data, and then hoping that you haven't been taken advantage of (While I am aware that there is a feedback system on such sites, and they may be more trustworthy than your back-alley ID craftman, you would have to do quite a bit of research to make sure they won't put you at risk in a way). Drugs have been the centerpiece of the dark net for a long time, it is one of the very few illegal things one can do without hurting anyone other than themselves. Be it cannabis, cocaine, ecstasy, opioids, or stolen prescription drugs, you can find them there, while some people may have to resort to such markets because of a mistake in the system, one not getting painkillers prescribed after a borderline fatal accident for example, oftentimes the reason for doing so is substance abuse, and not because it is necessary for their well-being.

Deception

There are three main groups of vocal members in the community of cryptocurrency users, that affect its public perception, even if some are rather insulated from the surface of it. These special groups artificially keep cryptic currencies' price up enough, and for time long enough to let them create magnificent amount of profit from such acts, before it eventually causing it to collapse on its own weight.

Socioeconomic – Political Effects

Criminals

One of the most malevolent to life, but healthy to the prices of the digital currencies are the criminals trying to find a common platform to exchange goods for, their optimal choice would most likely be Bitcoin, since it already has a strong backbone, while also possessing a big marginal market size potential. Such miscreant could employ a variety of techniques to manipulate the prices of cryptic currencies, one of them would be using "click farms" to spread the word about them, making the everyday person more likely to be more aware of such ways to spend their money. Doing so will incrementally increase the volume our criminal is able to trade without affecting, swaying the prices in any direction significantly, thanks to everyday people who wish to venture with their money as if they were playing darts, or betting on roulette in the middle of the desert in towns nobody has ever heard of. Since time immemorial crafty businessmen operating outside the reach of the law have always found ways to conduct business without using bank account transfers, or greenbacks, oftentimes it is as if we have gone back to the beginning of humanity at which we traded without a designated currency. Drug dealers always come up with a new good you may be able to find at your local grocery store, just so he or she can fulfill the needs of its substance dependent consumers, this list reaches from detergent, uncooked meat, to socks once again. See where I am going? Cryptic currencies are the equivalent to such goods, but for the people higher up in the food chain, with access to a certain amount of technology, enabling them to conduct business openly, as opposed to business at all when speaking for addictive substance salesmen. With such systems possibly being already employed, we will witness supplementary growth in size, artificially perceiving prices as higher, even if that may not have been the goal of the perpetrator, only to secure the exchange it was already using, consolidating it in a manner which benefits the consumer base, while also causing appealing growth to the general public. While such person may not be beneficial to society and the world as a whole, it is causing benign suffering to thousands, its works help the unaware investor tremendously by mitigating their worry of prices collapsing any moment by introducing continuous influx of fresh buyers to the market, and since the mentality of

Socioeconomic – Political Effects

unseasoned investors is could be ascribed to the exclamation "historical events predict the outcome of the future", it generates calm, and just let's in the hooshing of the wind in while you are trying to fall asleep, and not the roaring of a riot, alongside with an angry debt collector at your doorstep.

At this time there have not been openly acknowledged examples of such activities, however several states have taken notice that criminals often hide profits in the form of virtual currencies, making them practically untouchable on the site of unreported earnings. Such cases should not be surprising to us, since many cryptic currencies only hold their value because of their purchasing power, and not because of a derivable asset, or other redeeming feature.

Salesmen

There are many public figures who are established in the world of economics, preaching Bitcoin, telling you that only the sky is the limit, or that it is the currency to replace all others, often accompanied with the sayin' "All you have to do is have faith in it", but we all know how that turns out. Why would they be preaching something they (most likely) already know to be valueless? There is a practice under the title "pump 'n' dump" in the financial world, and often people who are caught in the act of doing it lose their credibility, and most likely, along with their fame. Therefore most often the acts are carried out insulated from them, by alternative accounts, using fake names, fake identities, and maybe even fake data, on forums, chatrooms, and other internet websites. But with cryptic currencies, they can tell the world about how great they are, how much money they made in a short time with it, the handiness it gives the user, and the list goes on with any and every possible way of selling an audience nonphysical things. What makes Bitcoin so different compared to other securities? What makes them able to commit such acts without the consequences? The answer to those questions is that cryptic currencies are still rather newfound to the public eye, so if they happened to crash, there would be no one to blame (maybe other than hard working bankers trying to save us from overvalued stocks) for it, and even if someone did accuse

Socioeconomic – Political Effects

someone of making false statements about Bitcoin, they could just claim that they missed a detail, and didn't quite understand the nature of such currencies. While many of us think sales methods don't work on us, and that we immediately notice if someone is trying to line their pocket with our money, it's best to keep in mind that the best ones actually believe their own lie(s), thereby go unnoticed even by the people usually aware of miscreants with similar intents. In the early days of the 20th century, these acts were popular amongst stock brokers, and leaders of companies, we have all seen movies about slick-haired salesmen selling a company's issue to unassuming people without telling them anything of important at all about the company's performance, this was fairly common to do back when the SEC had limited grip on securing the safety of the buyer from heinous acts, such as lying on financial statements. Nowadays (in the old days too) it is viewed as common practice for CEOs to say nothing but great things about the company they represent, it is something so commonly found that it cannot be considered "pump 'n' dump"-ing, it is practically included in their job description, and while there are many with bad intentions, executives that do not misinform people, do their job of moving the company forward without broadcasting it live to the world at all times still exist. We should be glad for such men and women in our world.

This method of influence will create a bull market, making prices shoot up since people are desperate to not miss out on the next big thing, seeing that prices have gone up violently in the past few weeks, days, even hours can cause them to act without thinking, just to make sure they are onboard and seated. There are many celebrities out there that swear by cryptic currencies, telling that the internet needs its own currency, and while that may be the case, most of it is not of malicious nature, similar goes for the economists, journalists telling the world about the thing without putting a "WARNING" sticker on the slip. Thankfully there have been several wealth preserving people spreading awareness on the dangers of such currencies, the presence of wrong in it, doing what they do causes the everyday person to be more vary of their investments and makes them pay a little bit more attention to the details, opening up a safer financial world for everyone involved, not to mention one with less heart / headache.

Socioeconomic – Political Effects

Bottom-Feeder

The third and last group that vocally influences the market by deception is quite similar to the previous example, but on a smaller scale. This type of person bought into Bitcoin with their savings, along with all their faith, it believes with all its heart that such currency can grow indefinitely, this creates a walking advertisement, telling everyone why it is so good, without a single good reason. People similar to this are the ones that you will bump into in chatrooms, witness on social networking sites, spreading the word about a security that can be worth more than all of the money printed in the world, just by putting your "trust" it. If we went by such methodology, we would end up with overinflated prices on companies that are worth close to nothing, along with wheat being sold for the price of gold. Now you see the problem with this type of behavior, basing one's beliefs on a weak foundation should not be worth close to $100B, even if you are able to buy cat pictures and cocaine with them. Such persons are comparable to slaves of a system, who feel as if they were doing it voluntarily without outside influence, they turn a blind eye to the illegal being of the cryptic currencies, and are desperate to confirm their beliefs on every material they can base it on, but I would still consider them not guilty, their only crime is not knowing enough.

There are many internet forums dedicated to functioning as something similar to a support group, but for cryptic currencies. A skeptic's words have never hurt anyone, and avoiding such spaces can benefit us to a great degree since hearing from more than one side helps us gain a greater perspective on things, that is one of the reasons schools exist, you meet people from all walks of life and while most of them do not have malevolent intentions, we can start believing false information if we do not scrutinize one's words thoroughly enough, and open up to other voice. It is a man's goal to always try to find out the opposite of what they know, and believe only the truth at the end of the day.

General Discussion & Views

The purpose of this segment of the book is to objectively sum up both the upsides, and the downsides of using cryptocurrencies. With the newfoundness of Bitcoin, not many things can be said with complete confidence, just based on & projected by previous events, studies conducted on different financial markets, and with differing probabilities still being kept in mind during the writing process. While by the word of mouth you might have heard exclusively great things, and only unfavorable from my part, I will attempt to give both sides an argument for what they stand for, and even though there are several smaller, yet comparatively unimportant topics that could be touched on, the chapter mostly focuses on what may affect the lives of average user, along with the overall perspective the everyday person has of cryptic currencies, therefore discussing such topics could affect the briefness of this piece of literature.

For

Versatility

Arguably, one of the greatest selling points of Bitcoin is its versatility, if you want to buy something, you can get it as long as someone is selling it, no matter the legality of such merchandise. Even though allegedly there are many non-criminal uses to it, most are of questionable intent, this unique trait makes it derive its perceived value from its purchasing power, making it have considerable value even without rock solid backing (Which is a somewhat new sensation in the financial world). Such valuation in the case of stocks would be detrimental to the future of the company, if a company had a Market Capitalization of over $1Billion, but no assets, or earnings of any kind, its price would fall faster than gravity could handle, on the contrary, it doesn't apply to Bitcoin since it has that special aura surrounding it, people will always strive to be able to use drugs in this world, as long as negative human emotions exist, along with currently

General Discussion & Views

unresolvable issues, people will want to ease the pain inside. The greatest non-criminal use for Bitcoins is avoiding headache-inducing financial systems, which could risk your personal information, along with your financials, therefore creating a separate entity to transact money to information creators, journalists, charities, or people in need is great practice if you are worried about people interceding with your transaction. Committing to transactions in such way can prevent people from selling your priceless data, and it also stimulates the earning power of the person you are sending coins to, which in other situations would have been something you wouldn't have thought of, but since you wield hundreds of dollars' worth of internet coins on your person at all times, that you can just pass along as if you walked down the street, tipping a street musician, artist, or the guy who pretends to be a frozen statue all day in the 110 degree weather for months during tourist season.

Moving Money

The ease of moving money with cryptic currencies is something that one would expect from their banking services, unfortunately it had to be a party like Bitcoin to popularize a method with which we can send money to relatives, friends, business partners all across the globe instantaneously, and with confirmations it is still less than one hour we have to account for when transporting money to others' accounts. Not only is it quick but it is also comparatively cheap since no one wants to suck the money out of our wallets as we send it to person in question, all we have to do is pay the transaction fee which is only existent to keep the incentive for blockchain workers, something we can live with and sacrifice for. One of the greatest advances we can attribute to cryptic currencies is the blockchain, this technology creates a decentralized financial system, meaning that people host a complete accounting ledger of all transactions on their computer in exchange for the cryptic currency it tracks, this is a cheap and effective way of avoiding nosy banking services who would take our money not in exchange for their services, but to line their pockets with silver.

General Discussion & Views

Taxation

While in most countries gains from growth in cryptocurrencies are treated as if they were from run of the mill investments, it takes quite a feat for the revenue service to find out if someone has realized profits from such investments, if they did not directly report it themselves. With it being relatively easy to do, even the everyday person might consider working outside the notice of government, only reporting fractions of the profits, using the rest for services they can gain access to through cryptic currencies, what they would have bought otherwise, but with money that the authorities cannot get ahold of. As mentioned earlier in this book, cryptocurrencies can be used to avoid unnecessary government interference, giving the user a clearer state of mind relating to their security of privacy, being able to avoid minor wrongdoings from diminishing their opportunity to create themselves a better future, but that is only possible with enough care, and respect for all entities involved. Such benefits might change depending on outside factors, if criminal organization gets well-known for using virtual currencies, politicians could find a reason to cause turmoil, not only limiting its ability to stay above the law, but possibly taking away from its perceived value. As much as the governments could affect the future of Bitcoins, just like so can its user base, if they use it with enough care as noted previously, they can preserve its well-being for a long time.

Counterfeiting

As one would expect it is nearly impossible to introduce money not approved by the body overlooking it to the system, in this case the blockchain, with Bitcoin having a limited supply and all of them being tracked we can know for sure that the money we are being wired is not of questionable quality, or material, with digital goods there is no difference between each product, they are all equal. Even though less than 1% of the money in circulation is counterfeit, every year there are countless dollars being spent on taking illicit money out of the system, which could have been spent on something more important. An amount smaller than one percent might appear small, but if fake dollar bills suddenly appeared in a small community, it would more than likely inflate the prices, causing honest to god, law-abiding people to draw the short stick, making them unable to buy luxury & high quality goods because of the unreasonably high prices, caused by miscreants.

Newfound

Newfound, unique, volatile. Three adjectives that can be used to describe Bitcoin, since they are currencies we haven't had much experience with previously, it is something everybody talks about, yet nobody knows what it is, this gives us the ability to still discover phenomenon in the market previously not apparent to us, many things to shed light on. With that in mind, it is extremely volatile, and if someone is careful and adept enough, they may be able to utilize the bull market's workings for their own good, and make "daytrading" viable to gain similar performances as to what we've witnessed in the early and rather exclusive days of the stock market. While still not advised, such short-term growth can practically make anyone with half-a-brain look like a stock market genius, but the only way to find out who has the proficiency to stay afloat, is to wait until the downturn comes and causes the said bright minds to shine, who have respected markets of similar temperatures from a far, and with complete respect, as opposed to the ones who overtraded, and abused their privileges. The mentioned growth may keep on beating the major indexes for a few more years, and if one is conservative enough with his or her investing, they may be able to come out on top in the end. We have witnessed several similar trends, and I would argue that this might be one of the few ones that can be rid by people who aren't necessarily lucky; they just have to have enough expertise, and be aware of their surroundings. Balance and not getting ahead of yourself are one of the few traits that help your get ahead in life, and you can teach yourself.

Resilient

One of the most precious qualities of cryptocurrencies is that they are not directly affected by outside changes in the market, if an index is down by several points, Bitcoin's price is not related to it at all, same goes for currency exchanges, since it is not connected to any governing body with an umbilical cord, any currency could leave the surface of earth, without affecting the value of coins noticably. While it is still a possibility that if a major country does something that diminishes its currency's value, the price of Bitcoin would go down with it significantly (e.g. United States starts printing billion dollar bills while an economic crisis happens), but as time goes on the only parameter that would be affected is the exchange rate against the said currency for a certain coin. It being so resilient is thanks to a practice called hedging, while there isn't a certain financial body at Bitcoin headquarters that strategically purchases certain portions of the market, along with popular currencies, it is a quality inherent to it, since it acts as something working outside the traditional practices of the financial world. The greatest known method to recession proof one's portfolio is to diversify, purchase stocks, bonds, commodities, not just in the country you are familiar with, but on the eastern side of the globe, in developing nations, the options are nearly endless. While it does sound exhausting to sweep through financial documents written in a language that you don't understand, and can't quite figure out how to use google translate to your advantage, there is a shortcut you can take, many mutual funds contain carefully selected & diversified securities from nations afar away, and you can just read the method by which they are selected, along with the expectations they have for it, this way you can choose one that matches what you have in mind without having to learn a new language. Since cryptocurrencies possess the ability to work in a fashion similar to this, it is something you are able to view as you would an index, but for the entire world's currencies, companies, and overall ability to work efficiently (theoretically).

Detached

With us being inherently out of the scope of the government, we should utilize it as much as we have to. Being outside the vision of certain bodies can benefit one greatly, as discussed in previous segments of the book, ranging from protecting personal freedom, to preserving the future of one's

General Discussion & Views

country. The ability to speak our minds is good. All that being said if we are not careful enough such liberties may be taken from us, by both our actions, and inaction. The excessive use of it for criminal purposes, selling and buying illicit goods could cause governing bodies to pass legislation which restricts one's ability to use anonymous currency. While leaderships might control the use of such currencies, not taking the right precautions when using our accounts can make our real-life selves vulnerable to being exploited, connected to the wallet we possess. Ways of this happening will be discussed in later sections.

General Discussion & Views

Against

Fundamentally Unstable

As discussed in great detail beforehand in this book, cryptic currencies do not possess any of the traditional qualities one would look for when purchasing a security, the only thing it has is a faithful, and overly excited crowd surrounding it. While it does have great recent growth (which some would consider a redeeming trait), we must still keep our eyes on the weakest points of it, examining them rigorously. It being a bubble that is not collectively recognized, poses great threat to the people who are interested in buying coins themselves, if they do not do enough research, or get caught up in the "hype", they are at risk of losing significant amounts of money. With enough people pretending that it is worth the price being paid for it, or even more, the prices will be kept in the higher price ranges, as if it as built on clouds, until people with more money than brains don't want to buy virtual currencies of this kind anymore, as the burning passion dies off in the people, so will the prices of coins. As noted in the first point made in this chapter, it is volatile, sometimes that can be considered good, but in most cases it is the other way around, if one was to buy a Bitcoin and forget about it, it would most likely have lost its value when they have remembered to look at it again, unlike with Stocks, Bonds, or any other type of established securities, with which you would have woken up to discover your money has either gained interest, or grown at a stable, yet constant rate.

Only Accepted by Few

At the present time cryptocurrencies are not widely accepted around the globe, be it by suppliers selling at wholesale prices, or simple merchants of everyday products. This problem arises from the fact that crpytocurrencies are extremely volatile, and difficult to liquidate, if a business were to receive 1000 Bitcoins, and wanted to exchange it for property worth 1000 coins, or liquidate it, they might end up losing money if the prices of the coins fluctuate in the wrong direction. Let's say the typewriter you have been using for the past decade started malfunctioning, therefore you decide to purchase a keyboard with similar qualities to the typewriter you had before, materials, spring weights, etcetera, but you are unable to find a vendor who sells the keyboard you had in mind & also accepts some form of cryptic currencies. The problem is that as more variables start to arise, the less likely it will be for you to find a merchant who is able to fulfill your needs. If you think this is an overly specific example, and such would not apply to you, imagine that you are outside and want to have a cappuccino, but once again you do not have any real money in your wallet, only Bitcoins, in such scenario you are left hanging, not being able to complete the transaction without leaving the café, and engaging in an uncomfortable dialogue with one of the employees. The reason they are difficult to liquidate is that there is no certain market for it, unlike with tobacco, wool, or ornaments during the colonial days of our country, if you had to, you could trade any of these commodities with most of the groups, even if they didn't have much use for it, they knew that there was someone out there in need of tobacco or wool in one of the other communities. With cryptic currencies, it could be classified as a deadlock, companies do not want to accept cryptic currencies in exchange for their services because they are not able to liquidate them in a short enough time, and this causes other companies to not intend to participate either, one of the very few industries that accept cryptic currencies are ones revolving around technology, the reason for this is that most transactions in computing can be done without having inventory, the only necessity for them is a product that can be sold over and over again.

Criminal use

Presumably, the most common use of cryptocurrencies is to buy illicit goods that are difficult to access with traditional money – through the internet, strictly speaking. While at first glance it might not be apparent, exercising such ways of transacting money lets criminals take control of us to a certain degree, the market for cryptocurrencies at the very least. If we purchase a coin just to hold onto it, thinking that we didn't buy it with criminal intent, most of that money will still anyway be used unbeknownst to us to line the pockets of drug dealers, and other criminals alike. This phenomenon even applies to some people who we would never even suspect of participating in criminal activities; money laundering is a practice not unheard of in its community, the encyclopedia of Bitcoin even gives you a detailed manual, as to how you should go on about doing so, while metaphorical "DANGER", "WARNING" and "DO NOT EVEN THINK ABOUT COMMITTING SUCH HENIOUS ACT" stickers are plastered all over the said pages. If you are still not quite convinced, saying that this is a free country, and that how people make their money should not be any of our concern, let me theoretically claim the said goods go somewhere near your place of living, if it is drugs, they could be consumed by people in your family if they are prone to doing so, potentially having detrimental effects on their life, or a crate of guns get shipped to an area near, increasing the amount of aggravated assaults, along with robberies, and even murder. While it is still quite a possibility that people wanting to buy such merchandise would have gotten it in another way, but millions of dollars are already being spent every year to prevent unnecessary lives from being ruined or taken, so why should we just look the other way when it comes to one of the greatest sources of illicit goods in our country?

Evaluation

We live in the golden-age of consumer safety when it comes to participating on the stock market, the Security Exchange Commission mandates that all companies of great enough size have to file reports showing their financial statement, balance sheet, risk factors, and several other qualities that are important to an investor who utilizes fundamental analysis. If a company lies on their documents, they can get punished severely for it, making the act of doing so detrimental to the people committing the fraud, and the people in leading positions at the company, who might not even have had anything to do with it. Many of the previous bubbles were caused by it being difficult to access information about the companies themselves, and even in cases where they could get information it was likely from your homely stock guide, which for the most part only included raw numbers, and rarely ever any other supplementary information (even though in most cases the raw data was sufficient for one's purpose, the text section still helps people find & weed out the companies with internal problems). The revolution of information being readily accessible gave practically anyone the opportunity to begin honing their skills at financial analysis, but oftentimes the crowd surrounding them discourages the action of doing so, which is something we should get past, since it limits the awareness of the average person, when discussing the backbone of companies.

Different suit, but of the same kind

This problem applies to most real-life currencies as well, there are so many currencies in the world that it would take too much effort to count them all, but this problem arose from the world not being connected to everything and everyone at all times, however with cryptic currencies it is done voluntarily, with the community enabling it. There are as many greedy people with no real talents, sense of business, as there are variations of Bitcoin, very few of them supply the end-user with something that would enhance their experience, or let them do something they would not have been able been able to do otherwise, the greatest comparison I can make is those additional coins are functioning as if they were dedicated to do one thing, and that only (The only exception I was able to find let the user be nearly completely anonymous, though this can be done with Bitcoin if you do your preparations, making such features nearly completely useless), it is as if they were created just to exist and suck money out of careless people's pockets, the ones who are desperate to attempt hop on to the next big thing, even if they are an hour late, unfortunately for them, such is not likely to happen if they are expecting performances similar to Bitcoin's, ending up picking at bread crumbles instead of taking the expected pie.

Security Issues

Building on the final point made in the "For" argument, while it is detached from your real life self, if you are not attentive enough, an investigative person might be able to connect you to your account, potentially landing you in jail. Let's say you buy some Cuban cigars from vendor #1, and then go on to order some forged documents to the address at which you reside at, in your own name... etcetera, from a merchant who happens to be a police informant unit disguised as someone selling forgeries, in some cases they even deliver the documents, either with a surprise or they keep their eye on you for a while after the delivery has taken place. Now they have enough evidence to put you in jail for two charges, purchasing contraband, and possibly identity theft, all thanks to the methodology used in the blockchain, anyone can view the flow of coins from the public ledger, possibly stringing you to your address, all it takes is one mishap to land you incarcerated. With that in mind, if you are careful enough and take the proper precautions, it could be very difficult for you to incriminate yourself accidentally.

Security

Cryptic currencies, especially Bitcoin, are extremely well-thought out and well-known for their invulnerability to mass attacks, in some cases being even more secure than the technology used by banks, all thanks to the "blockchain", a public ledger distributed amongst users, confirming transactions as time goes by (around every 10 minutes / Block of confirmations). Breaking such method of keeping records would require one to have enormous amounts of computing power, and even if a miscreant managed to top off such feat, it would be almost certainly unprofitable for it, they could gain more if they worked with the system instead, and most likely, plugged the electronics out, since maintaining and providing electricity for such infrastructure would cost unbelievable amounts in just variable costs. With this being said, although mass attacks are impossible to orchestrate according to our current knowledge, attacks on single entities could still be executed, similar to criminals gaining access to one's banking information or other financials.

Encryption

Encryption is one of the essential tools one has to utilize to maximize their security when using computer software, to say the least, if it wasn't useful to have the military wouldn't use it either, and while most newer clients come with such features integrated, it still has to be emphasized that if it isn't the case, eavesdroppers can relatively easily interrupt transactions, and so could programmers with criminal intent steal your coins if they managed gain access to your computer one way or another. Lack of integrated anonymity is also a concern, your IP address isn't hidden unless you use an external program to hide such information, a VPN for example, but even then the history of coins can be linked to your wallet, and that very account can be linked to merchants of illicit goods, landing you in jail if an entity manages to connect all of them together. There are some ways that you can practically erase the history of your coins, however most if not all of them are quasi-coin-laundering methods, which can be deemed illegal by the court of law if not done carefully, or in the proper circumstances.

E-Wallets

There are several E-Wallet services that pool your coins with others' and let you withdraw them at your request, such services are useful if you want to be able to access your coins while away from your desktop computer, on the road, or under any circumstances that restrict your ability access to your cryptic currencies, or you just want to keep them all in the same place for some reason (Most clients do not allow you to keep more than just one type of coin in your wallet). Such websites could be compared to online security holding sites, which allow you to purchase from stock exchanges, and participate in financial activities without having to go through a rigorous process, just to be able to conduct such business, however as opposed to services like that, E-Wallets generally are not legally obliged to perpetuate their business with you, making them liable to be able to run off with your coins unexpectedly. This could be classified as overnight risk, since if you do not read enough into the site's terms of service and else, or research them well enough to mitigate the risk of the webservice committing potentially illegal actions, harming you along with others, if it were to happen it could in a warped way be your fault, since you could have prevented great harm being done to others, at little cost to yourself (unless you value your time more than the amount of securities stored on such websites).

Wallets

As with online wallets, wallets stored on your hard drive can get compromised if you are unlucky & inattentive enough. One of the most common causes of damage is done by corrupted disks, if the computer you are using for your cryptocurrency needs has an old storage drive, maybe one that has been disfigured by external forces (or by pure chance, if it is still young and damage-free it still has a slim chance of passing away), you may be at high risk that your disk gives up, leaving files corrupted, potentially leaving you hopeless in recovering your coins if you were not careful

Security

enough (haven't backed up your data). Another similar case is if you were to change your client's password, and something happened to your computer, it gets compromised, or you just exchange it for a new one, you won't be able to use the old backup of the wallet to regain access to it, since changing the password on a wallet is similar to changing accounts, and just floating the coins over to the new one, you wouldn't be able to access the new one with the old one's credentials. The lesson that can be learned from such scenarios is that if you are in doubt, back your data up, that way you are able to sleep with a clear mind.

Malicious Client

If there is a person with evil intent, great programming, marketing skills, enough time and resources, they could potentially create a cryptocurrency client, which could under the right certain circumstances strip you of your coins. For one to execute such feat, they would first would have to create a client, similar to the ones you may be used to seeing used by others, or you may even have one yourself, but it would have to be different in several ways, it either has to be closed-source, or have the malovent code written in a cluttered, unintelligible, yet still subtle (similar to the code used to present the miscellaneous workings of the program) fashion, while also fulfilling the functions one would expect from such clients, possibly even having a quality which would make it look apart, more desirable, better compared to alternatives. The second step they would have to do is sell it, not to umbrella / holding companies, but to users, the people who would like to possess coins themselves, achieving this could be done by using clickfarms, paying people from developing nations to spread the word about the amazing program, or by networking, working with other developers (while attempting to stay anonymous) to build reciprocity, benefitting both of you in the end. When one has amassed a big enough userbase, with enough coins, and is ready to cash out on his / her venture, they could either export the coins in fractions, as transactions flow, the people with great amounts of coins who constantly keep their number of coins above a certain threshold would have the coins taken from them, while it still appears as if it held the believed amount. The other option being packing your bags, and taking all

Security

coins out of circulation at once, giving the users little to no notice as to what happened, as you distribute your coins in several separate accounts and start laundering them, and finally, laundering the money you have received from executing such plan.

Conclusion

If the problems described in previously in this book were to be solved, or mitigated to a greater degree, we could begin treating Bitcoin as a real currency, security which we could purchase as a way to extend, or broaden our portfolio, without being speculative outside our control. For cryptic currencies to become autonomous, free of artificial interference from outside bodies, it has to achieve a certain set of qualities which help us establish that it is priced at a reasonable level, some of which can be accelerated by its user base, aiding the rate at which it progresses towards accomplishing such attributes. With some, or most of such goals met, cryptic currencies could become a new class of non-speculative securities, which can be used with prudent intent, researched, analyzed, and worked with in a way that benefits not just the economy, but society aswell. But as long as we exist in a world full of imperfections, we must look at it from a perspective similar to Philip J. Kaplan's, someone who would most likely describe cryptic currencies in a similar manner:

I send a stranger 10% of my annual salary

They give me a valueless "Bitcoin", which can be only used to buy things that a law-abiding man doesn't even think about

The smart people (who might have manipulated the market) sell off their accumulated cryptic currencies on an exchange, causing the prices to fall faster than a cinder block that has been dropped off the highest point of a tower

I am left with no money, my wife filing for divorce, all because I believed everything the internet told me.

Conclusion

Qualities

Stability, one of the main factors that have to be examined when looking at the safety of a security, if a cryptic currency has gone a year without any violent, unreasonable price surges or declines, one can only assume that the overexcitement has died down, and that we can safely begin to work with such works. As with stocks, one year's data would not tell us much about the overall state of such securities, but we have to keep in mind that cryptocurrencies are still relatively young, and one year is just enough time to make a crude assumption about their current state, as time goes on we can look at the bigger picture and have a clearer vision, understanding of the workings of such articles. After Bitcoin starts exhibiting signs of stability, the next parameter we should be paying attention to is growth, it cannot be more effective in earning than the major indexes around the world, however it can't be slower than the rate of inflation (1-2-5%) of leading currencies around the globe (USD – CHF – KYD – EUR – JPY - GBP) either. A comparatively slow (to our current situation), yet steady growth is healthy for everyone involved in the usage of the currency, saving many from the headaches caused by unexpected intra-day price swings, while restricting the rate at which it can grow, preventing bubbles from surfacing once again. For them to be able to be autonomous, the leaderships of major countries have to agree, and state that they will not pass legislation against cryptocurrencies, this can provide a clearer state of mind, and mitigate the worrying of attentive people involved in the trading of cryptic currencies. The stances of countries on coins will soon be revealed since they grow at exorbitant rates at this moment, both on charts, and in the minds of the citizens of the countries mentioned, governing bodies expressing such opinions could allow cryptocurrencies to overcome the obstacles, challenges it currently faces, the ones preventing it from acting as an everyday security. As such traits get recognized, constant flow & exchange between cryptocurrencies and commodities could arise, similar to the fiat backed money we are familiar with today, they had some sort of backing before only their country stood behind them, with cryptic ones it could have been the hype that was used as its training wheels, not gold or some other precious metal. An established trade rate would be similar to interlocking

Conclusion

while kitting, one feeds off of the other, creating a domino effect where everything is priced at its optimal value, thanks to a mysterious invisible power.

Actions

The incentive for us to achieve a healthy market that is not at risk of anyone interceding, is the end goal itself, promoting safe ways of working with the market is beneficial to everyone participating, making it predictable & stable is considered a priceless quality in almost any contemporary market. Preemptively we should discourage the using cryptic currencies for the purchasing of illegal goods (promoting taxation), and encourage using it for everyday activities instead, if it stops becoming the primary use of coins, the likelihood of legislature being passed against drops significantly, while consumer confidence increases along with the credibility of cryptocurrencies. We all know how much the federal government spends every day just to prevent criminal activities from taking place, and if they wanted to make a simple statement to abolish one of the greatest obstacles in doing so, they could commit to doing so at any moment, but if the everyday person (non-criminal) was considered to be the majority of its users, and the ones using it for selling illicit goods and services weren't so prominent, we could probably sleep better at night. Not to mention that the normal person realizing profits on such investments is likely to report it, and we should still urge everyone to not hide it unless necessary, a la they live in a state where gaining wealth through questionable means and reporting it gains unnecessary attention. For some there are ethical / moral reasons to give a cut of their income to the government, or some other body, if one has that inner need to help others, I recommend you visit your nearest church and donate the surplus to them, or if you are not religious in any way, do it through a charity, but do not forget to research them beforehand to make sure that the money is going to people in need, and not people who want to line their pockets. Theoretically a small governing body could be elected for cryptic currencies to help the user base stay up to date, help with government relations, future goals, maybe even promote, establish constant trading rates or select commodity / service to use as backing. One of the

Conclusion

possible basic services which could be used as backing would be Virtual Private Network subscriptions, if major companies wanted to help cryptic currencies find the lowest possible value which providers would accept in exchange, they could accomplish several things while only doing one, by purchasing a period-long VPN for every member of the company, they do not only improve the privacy accompanied to their workings, but also help Bitcoin get a baseline value. Another example would be using computer parts, CPUs, Drives, or any other high demand component which with time has to be replaced. While such happenings are not necessary to create a functioning currency, it sure is beneficial to have something subsidiary to use as backing when recognized collectively, but in case some sort of backing is not able to be found, cryptic currencies may find minimal values one by one for goods, feeding off of one-another, just like with fiat money, but in such scenario it will take longer at the very least. The main goal of studying such currencies is to prevent instruments from becoming severely overpriced, but unfortunately it is too late to give its users notice, so now we have to settle for the second best thing in attempt to mitigate the bubble, decreasing the price of it slowly, making it so that it reaches a level in a year or two where it is at an acceptable price, representing its usable value. For such phenomena to happen, collective realization of the real value of such security is difficult to execute, therefore we have to establish that we are dealing with a mature crowd that can be worked with without causing crisis before proceeding, but in other cases the procedure that works well is selectively doing choosing a portion of the user base, reasoning with them about the perceived value of such products, doing so won't cause a widespread calamity affecting many reckless investors who bought into such because of pressure or mere gut feels, but instead gives them a window big enough for them to close their standing.

When qualities promoting healthy market environments arise, the next objective one should aim for is to be able to quantitatively analyze the market revolving around cryptic currencies, being able to tell the value of a security without trusting the price tag on it is the reason why some people wake up for in the morning. Established methods for fundamentally analyzing companies are still changing slightly every now and then, similar

Conclusion

can be said about other types of securities, and while some of them rely heavily on technical & event-based analysis, I personally believe that cryptic currencies could be fundamentally analyzed, by looking at raw data, instead of starting at senseless candles, or the news. One of the proposed methods of conducting business in such manner would be to look at how much of selected cryptocurrencies are being traded for certain goods around the world, at what price, etcetera. This will be made possible as more and more companies start collecting & keeping data on their transactions with Bitcoin, and in the process we will be able to find more methodologies to be used one way or another. A clearer understanding of cryptic currencies as a whole could provide future markets with the knowledge needed to not reenact the mistakes we have committed in the early days of crypto, while our foresight is legally blind, we can learn from the past events in these fields, and remember that fixing mistakes is much more difficult than not having done them at all in the first place. We don't only need a select few to have a clear understanding of the financial works of securities, but preferably every person who's looking to diversify their portfolio, since they are the ones spending the most money on coins, but this is probably too much to ask for, the stock market is well over one hundred years old and quite a bit of the participants don't understand the methods of analysis which could lead to them having a secure, interest gaining portfolio, yet they are still too stubborn to turn to professionals for help. While human-proofing the markets is practically impossible, we should also strive for completely security in our clients, put all workings of it under extreme scrutiny, and attempt to eliminate, minimalize every security risk one can think of, since in case cryptocurrencies become something traded on a day to day basis by professionals, corporations, it would be quite damaging to our perspective, and society if someone managed to find a weakness and exploit it because someone of clear conscience didn't find, or notice the said weakness.

End

Final Words

I have wondered a lot on whether or not should I be disclosing my thoughts on as to what should one do when they find that my writing opposes them in a way or another, but I have come to the conclusion that leaving it out could be severely detrimental to my mental and physical health to a great degree.

In case a government agency feels as if my writing is an obstacle for them (that is the usage of cryptic currencies is a necessity, and they have already amassed great amounts of it), preventing them from accomplishing something tremendously important, that could greatly endanger the future of their country, the U.S., or make them unable to discover something revolutionary, I recommend you contact me through an U.S. agency, with great amounts of information supplied. As long as you come peacefully, and aren't impatient, I would be happy to cooperate with your cause. If you were put in a situation where you must come in contact with me (in public), please do so in an area where at least 10 people are present in a 100 yard radius.

If you are an individual, or an organization, someone whose line of work greatly relies on the usage of cryptic currencies, and possesses significant amounts of it, you may also have a way of getting in contact with me, by using the following email address: dealcontact177@protonmail.com.

I would greatly enjoy if you aswell provided great amounts of information about your activities, with which I can determine whether or not does the price of cryptic currencies really affect a greater cause. Please do not contact me in person until further instructions are given. Please do not engage in illegal activities in attempt to preserve your own wealth, I am aware as to how easy it is to inflict great damage on a person through the internet if you have enough money.

I am a diplomatic person who prefers peace to violence.

Sincerely –

Support the author: 12p9C1HY3eBipou4ABVXngMXso6Vv3w65t

Donate to a Kay's suit fund: 37F7aHq2pokXjiAhLbBpoYfs6KvaJWwnSv

www.ingramcontent.com/pod-product-compliance
Lightning Source LLC
Chambersburg PA
CBHW050247230526
45470CB00005B/2152